EDO ACCESSORIES

HIRANO Hideo

SHOGAKUKAN

Bilingual Guide to Japan
EDO ACCESSORIES

HIRANO Hideo

Book and Cover design ©Kindaichi Design

Published by
SHOGAKUKAN
2-3-1 Hitotsubashi Chiyoda-ku,
Tokyo 101-8001 JAPAN
https://www.shogakukan.co.jp
https://japanesebooks.jp/en/

EDO KOMONO BILINGUAL GUIDE by
HIRANO Hideo
©2021 Hideo Hirano, Kazuhiro Uchida/
SHOGAKUKAN
Printed in Japan
ISBN 978-4-09-388846-2

江戸小物バイリンガルガイド

平野英夫 監修

小学館

English Renderings of Edo Accessories

This English and Japanese bilingual book introduces the basic knowledge and representative types of Edo accessories.

All Japanese terms are rendered in italicized Roman characters. The only diacritical mark used is the hyphen.

Since the conventions for rendering these terms into English differ depending on the facility, terms used elsewhere may not be consistent with those used in this book. Given that even Japanese names and pronunciations may differ depending on the sect or region, they cannot be generalized. Standard names are used in this book and are rendered so that they can be easily read by individuals who are not native speakers of Japanese.

本書の英文表記について

この本は、代表的な江戸小物について紹介しています。日本語が母語ではない人のために、英語で訳してあります。

日本語はすべてローマ字読みにし、斜体のアルファベットで表記しています。発音しにくい長い単語はハイフン(−)を使用しています。

※これら外国語表記は、施設（公共施設、地方自治体等）ごとに異なるルールで表記されているため、本書と一致しない場合があります。地方によって日本語でも呼び方が異なることがあり、一般化はできません。本書では標準的な呼称を掲載し、外国語を母語とする読者ができるだけ平易に発音できる表記としました。

Table of Contents 目次

Introduction

Edo, One of the Largest Cities in the World

The Edo period (1603-1867) was a time of feudal rule, when the military (samurai) ran the government. In a military system, the shogun, or general, ranks at the top. The first shogun of the Edo period was Tokugawa Ieyasu (p. 104), and by hereditary succession, his descendants inherited his position. The shogun set the policies of the shogunate, or feudal government, and ruled over the 300 *daimyo* (p. 105) lords scattered throughout the country.

Kyoto, home to the emperor, remained as the nation's capital during the Edo period. Meanwhile, Edo (present-day Tokyo), home to the shogun, became the hub of politics, economy, and culture. In this hub lived samurai, craftsmen, merchants, and masses more, which by the 18th century turned Edo into one of the largest cities in the world, its population over one million.

はじめに

●江戸は世界最大級の都市だった

江戸時代（1603〜1867）は、軍事にたずさわる武士（侍）が政治を行った時代。武士階級の最高位は将軍で、初代将軍の徳川家康（p.104）の子孫が世襲で将軍の地位を受け継いだ。将軍は幕府（武士政権の政治機関）でさまざまな政策を決定して、全国に約300名いる大名（p.105）に命令した。

江戸時代の日本の首都は、天皇の住まいのある京都だったが、政治・経済・文化の中心は、将軍の居城のある江戸（現在の東京）だった。江戸の町には武士、職人、商人など多くの人びとが暮らし、18世紀の初頭には100万人超える世界最大級の都市となった。

Popular Culture Stimulated by Peaceful Times

The approximately 270 years of the Edo period were a time of peace, when social stability encouraged economic activity. On an individual level, the average person acquired personal wealth while indulging in their free time and their particular interests. In the area of entertainment, kabuki developed as a popular stage art. Theaters subsequently emerged in big cities such as Edo, Kyoto, and Osaka, as did a good many famous actors. Ukiyo-e prints depicted those actors and the urban mode of the day in arresting multicolor prints. The notion of urban culture spread when travelers to Edo gifted those prints to the rural folks back home.

The busy area outside the gate of a temple or shrine is known as a *monzen machi* (lit. a town in front of the gate). The famous *monzen machi* of Edo fanned out from the Asakusa district and included the licensed Yoshiwara (p. 106) pleasure quarters. This expanded entertainment area became the pulse point of trendsetting outfits and accessories.

●平和な時代が大衆文化を発達させた

　江戸時代は約270年にわたって平和な時代が続いた。世の中の安定は経済活動をさかんにし、一般の人びとも富を蓄えて余暇や趣味を楽しむようになった。娯楽では民衆の演劇として歌舞伎が発達し、江戸や京都、大坂などの大都市に常設の芝居小屋が置かれ、多くの名優が生まれた。これらの役者や当時の風俗を多色刷りの版画で描いたのが浮世絵である。地方から江戸に来た人びとはお土産として浮世絵を故郷に持ち帰り、都市文化の地方への伝播に一役買った。

　江戸には門前町から発展した浅草や、公認の遊郭のあった吉原（p.106）などの名所があり、これらの遊興地は服装やアクセサリーなど、流行の発信地となった。

High Fashion

In the latter half of the Edo period, *Edokko* (lit. child of Edo) men, proud of their Edo born and bred background, began to strut tobacco pouches and pipes that matched their demanding taste. The wealthiest of them indulged in bespoke accessories to show up what they considered arrogant samurai. Craftsmen upped their skills to fulfill the orders, and in the process, evolved into master artisans.

In the world of women, ladies-in-waiting who served at palaces of shogun and *daimyo*, in addition to wives of high-ranking samurai, adorned their hair with ornaments of exquisite materials. Not to be outdone, women of lower status, who belonged to merchant families, strutted their own intricate and ornate hair ornaments.

●よそおいの美

　江戸時代の後期になると、「江戸っ子」といわれる、江戸に生まれ育ったことを自負する男たちが、装身具の「たばこ入れ」「きせる」といった持ち物にこだわりを見せるようになる。彼らのなかでも裕福な者は、威張っている武士たちへの対抗心から、贅沢な素材を使ったオーダーメイドの装身具を注文した。これらの注文にこたえることで、職人の技術も向上し、多くの名工が生まれた。

　女性の世界では、将軍や大名などの御殿に仕える女性や上級武士の妻女たちが高級素材を用いた質の高い髪飾りをつけ、裕福な商家の女性らは緻密な細工を施した華やかな髪飾りで美を競った。

A Resurging Appreciation of Edo Accessories

During the Edo period, Japan conducted trade with the Netherlands and China in Nagasaki prefecture on the southern island of Kyushu. Imported raw materials, previously rare in Japan, were fashioned into accessories that soon became flamboyant. The shogunate frequently legislated against the possession of ostentatious kimono and other showy possessions. They reasoned it a social offense for commoners to possess anything beyond the means of a samurai. Commoners, on the other hand, still managed to enjoy their opulence with clever amounts of sidestepping, like lining their kimono with exotic fabric.

When the Edo period ended and Westernization proceeded into the Meiji period (1868-1912), ukiyo-e and the fine craftsmanship of Edo were dismissed as old-fashioned and low class. As a result, a massive number of art objects slipped abroad. But now, with a renewed appreciation of their artistry and techniques, enthusiasts of those art objects abound at home and abroad.

●見直される装身具の価値

　江戸時代の日本は、オランダと中国との貿易を長崎で行っていた。舶来の珍奇な素材は小物や装身具に用いられ、贅沢な作品が生まれた。いっぽうで幕府はたびたび奢侈禁止令を出して、贅沢な着物や持ち物を禁じた。庶民が武士階級よりも高価なものを所有することは身分制度に反するとみられたからである。しかし、人びとは着物の裏地を豪華にするなど、さまざまな工夫をしておしゃれを楽しんだ。

　江戸時代が終わり、明治時代に西洋化が進むと、浮世絵や小物工芸などは旧時代の低俗なものとみなされた。その結果、作品が海外へ大量に流出したこともあったが、現在は、高い芸術性や精緻な技術が見直され、国内外に多くの愛好家がいる。

Chapter 1

Omamori

第一章

お守り

History of *Omamori*

Omamori are pieces of wood or paper (*ofuda*) inscribed with the names or images of the deities, which are believed to be infused with the protective power of the gods.

Amulets have long been venerated in the home, high on altars, walls or pillars, or carried around on the person. For carrying around, however, amulet bags were devised to avoid wear and tear on the wood or paper *ofuda*. Although it is unclear when they first came into use, brocaded amulet bags that once belonged to aristocrats of the Heian period (794-1185) remain among the artifacts preserved today. Characteristic then was the *kake-mamori*, or hanging amulet, encased in a slim bag and tied at both ends with a stretch of cord to wear from the neck. From the aristocrats, the practice spread to the samurai class in the Kamakura period (1185-1333).

お守りの歴史

　お守りは、木片や紙片（お札）に神仏の名、絵やしるしなどを書いたもので、神仏の力によって身が守られると信じられる。

　お守りは家の神棚や仏壇に安置したり、家の壁や柱に貼ったりするほか、ふだんから身につけて携帯することも古くからおこなわれていた。木片や紙片はそのままでは難しいため袋に入れて携帯するのが一般的で、その袋を守袋と呼ぶ。守袋の起源は定かではないが、平安時代に貴族が所持していた錦織の守袋が現存している。守袋の両端に紐をつけて首から下げる形式にしたものを「懸守り」といい、はじめは貴族が用い、鎌倉時代になると武士層に広がった。

Omamori of the Edo Period

In the Edo period, once pilgrimages to holy sites, such as the *Ise Mairi* (p. 106), increased among the commoners, amulets from the Ise Shrine in Mie prefecture and other iconic places of worship rose in popularity.

The *kake-mamori*, which originally hung from the neck, hampered movement when it hit the chest. For comfort, it evolved into a crossbody type. Other types of amulets include *mune-mamori*, or chest amulets that can be tucked into the front folds of a kimono, *mamori-kinchaku*, or drawstring good luck pouches for children, in addition to *ude-mamori*, or arm amulets, worn, as described, on the arm.

The wealthy added color to the religious life of the townspeople in the luxurious fabrics of their made-to-order amulet pouches.

江戸時代のお守り

江戸時代になると伊勢まいり（p.106）をはじめとして、庶民の寺社詣でが盛んになるにともない、お守りは庶民に広く浸透した。

本来、懸守りは首から下げるものだったが、袋が胸に当たると動きがとりづらいことから、首から脇へ掛ける形式もあらわれた。そのほか、衣服の懐に入れる「胸守り」や、守袋を巾着形にした子供用のお守りの「守り巾着」、二の腕につける腕輪状の「腕守り」もある。

富裕層は高級な生地でつくった守袋を特注するなど、お守りの装いは江戸時代の庶民の信仰生活に彩りを添えた。

Hanging Amulet
Edo Period

Among the amulets in this bag of imported wool are an etching of the statue of Buddha from the Senso-ji Temple in Asakusa, Tokyo, an *ofuda* from the Ise Shrine, and a small scroll. The outer covering is of precious imported fabric, with the pattern of an imaginary sacred bird. A string of rare glass beads forms the strap.

懸守り　江戸時代
　羅紗の守袋の中に浅草寺の摺仏（印刷した仏像）や伊勢神宮のお札、小さな巻物などのお守りを入れている。守袋を納める外入れの生地は舶来の渡来裂で、想像上の霊鳥の絵柄。懸け紐はガラスビーズを紐状につないだ珍しいもの。

Toyohara Kunichika,
Ichikawa Kodanji as Toji (1863)
Kabuki actor, Ichikawa Kodanji,
opening a *kake-mamori*.

Utagawa Kunisada,
Ichimura Uzaemon as
Tobi-no-mono Shirataki
Sakichi (1860)
Kabuki actor,
Ichimura Uzaemon,
wearing a crossbody
kake-mamori.

Tubular Amulet
Edo Period

Another hanging variety was the *tsutsu-mamori,* a tubular amulet used by Heian period aristocrats. It consisted of a cylindrical piece of wood, such as bamboo, split down the middle to insert a talisman, then refitted back into a whoe. Later in the early modern period, cylinders were also produced in metal. The pouch shown here is of silk brocade, embossed with a *unryu,* or cloud-dragon, pattern.

東洲斎写楽筆「四代目岩井半四郎　重の井」
寛政6年（1794）〈複製〉
右手に筒守りを持つ。

Toshusai Sharaku, *Iwai Hanshiro IV as Shigenoi* (1794)
Kabuki actor, Iwai Hanshiro IV, holding a *tsutsu-mamori*
in his right hand.

筒守り　江戸時代

　懸守りのなかでも筒状の容器の形式を筒守りと呼ぶ。平安時代の貴族が用いたものは、筒状の木材を二つに割り、中にお守りを入れて合わせたものを用いた。近世になると金属製の筒守りもつくられた。守袋の生地は錦織で、雲龍の絵柄。

Arm Amulets
Late Edo Period

Arm amulets were popular in the *karyukai* (p. 107) world. The prototype can be traced back to the Kofun period (ca. 250-552), to what was known as a *kushiro,* a variety of armlet crafted from metal or seashells.

The Edo version, on the other hand, was fashioned from imported wool, crepe, chintz, or other types of fabric. A paper amulet was placed inside a slim, tube-like sack and looped into an armband. In a slightly different take, lovers, as well as geisha and their patrons, wrote the name of their significant other on a tiny piece of paper, which they placed inside the armband.

腕守り　江戸時代後期

　腕守りは江戸時代に花柳界 (p.107) などで流行った腕輪タイプのお守り。原型は古墳時代に、金属や貝でつくった「釧」という腕輪の一種といわれる。

　腕守りは羅紗、縮緬、更紗などの布を袋状の帯に仕立て、中に紙片のお守りを入

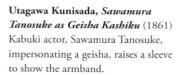

歌川国貞筆「沢村田之助　芸者かしく」
文久元年（1861）
袖をたくし上げて腕守りを見せる芸者。

Utagawa Kunisada, *Sawamura Tanosuke as Geisha Kashiku* (1861)
Kabuki actor, Sawamura Tanosuke, impersonating a geisha, raises a sleeve to show the armband.

れた。また、恋仲の男女や客と芸者が、たがいの名前を書いた紙片を入れて腕につけることもあった。

Good Luck Pouches
Late Edo Period

Amulets like these were tied to a child's *obi* (kimono sash) to ensure the offspring's hale and hearty growth. To give luck a helping hand, a piece of paper with the child's name and address was sometimes inserted with the talisman, if ever the child got lost. And for good measure, auspicious flowers and birds, carp swimming upstream against a waterfall (symbolizing bravery), as well as family crests, decorated the *kinchaku* pouch.

守り巾着　江戸時代後期
　守り巾着は子供の健やかな成長を願ってつくられたお守りで、子供の帯にくくりつけられた。巾着の中にはお守りのほかに、迷子になったときのために名前や住所を書いた紙を入れることもあった。巾着の絵柄は、花鳥や鯉の滝登りなどの縁起のいい絵柄や家紋があしらわれた。

Good Luck Pouch
Taisho Period

A child's *hanten* (p. 107) jacket, dating back to the Taisho period (1912-26), emblazoned on the back with the Japanese word for "festival." A good luck pouch of scarlet wool hangs from the lionhead *netsuke* perched atop the *obi*. Bright and festive in design and color, likely custom ordered by well-to-do parents.

守り巾着　大正時代

　背に大きく「祭禮」と染められた子供用の祭半纏（p.107）。帯に守り巾着が吊るされている。根付は獅子頭で、巾着は緋色の羅紗。祭にふさわしい派手な仕立てであることから、裕福な家の子供用につくられた特注品と思われる。

Fire Precaution
End of the Edo Period

Of the fires that occurred frequently in Edo, one of the most massive was the Great Fire of Meireki, which claimed more than 100,000 lives in 1657. To avoid such catastrophes, temples and shrines issued paper *ofuda*, exhorting people to "guard against fires." These were posted in household kitchens or on pillars, or mounted on scrolls.

火の用心　江戸時代末期

　10万人以上の死者を出した「明暦の大火」(1657) をはじめとして、江戸では火事が頻発した。人びとは火事を起こさぬように、寺社から授与される「火の用心」のお札を厨房の柱に貼ったり、軸装にして掛けたりした。

Altar for the Armor

Edo Period

This is a miniature Buddhist altar that a samurai would enfold into his armor before going off into battle. A tiny, but intricately carved and *kirikane* (p. 108) decorated statue of the Fudo Myo-o, the Wisdom King Acala, stands at the center, flanked by his attendants, Seitaka Doji on the left, and Kongara Doji on the right.

<hr />

鎧仏　江戸時代

　合戦に出る武士が、仏の加護を願って鎧の中に入れた小さな仏像。この像は厨子に納めた不動明王。小像でありながら精緻な彫りで、切金 (p.108) を施している。厨子の扉には、不動明王の従者の制吒迦童子 (写真左) と矜羯羅童子 (右) を描いている。

Chapter 2

Netsuke

第二章

根付

History of *Netsuke*

Sagemono is a category of personal items that includes *kinchaku* drawstring pouches, tobacco sets, and *inro* (p. 108), portable enough to be hung from a cord. A *netsuke* is tied to the other end of the cord to prevent the *sagemono* from falling when the cord is hung from the *obi*.

Netsuke are presumed to have come into use in the 17th century, sometime between the late Warring States period (1467-1615) and the early Edo period. Initially, natural materials such as bamboo ridges, shells, and ivory, cut into circles across the diameter, served that purpose. By the mid-Edo period, sculptors of Buddhist statues and casters began adding *netsuke* as a sideline to their business, gradually heightening it into an intricate art form. Then in the heyday of the townsmen culture known during the Edo period as Bunka-Bunsei (early 19th century), *netsuke* complemented the aesthetics of the luxurious *sagemono* they accompanied.

根付の歴史

　巾着、たばこ入れ、印籠 (p.108) など、紐で吊るして携帯する入れ物を「提物」という。根付は提物の紐の先端に付けられた留具で、帯の下から通し、帯の上に固定して提物が落ちないようにするものである。

　根付が使われはじめたのは戦国時代後期から江戸初期頃と考えられており、当初は竹の節や貝殻、象牙を輪切りにしたものなど、天然の素材を根付として利用した。その後、江戸中期になると仏師や鋳物師などが本業の傍ら根付をつくるようになり、次第に細密工芸品となってゆく。そして町人文化が爛熟した文化文政期を迎えると、贅を凝らした提物にふさわしい精巧な根付が根付専門の工人によってつくられるようになった。

Materials and Design of *Netsuke*

Most *netsuke* were carved from wood or ivory, boxwood being the most popular wood. Although ivory, as an import, commanded high prices, its carvability made it the craftsmen's choice. Stand-ins for ivory included walrus and wild boar tusks, in addition to deer and buffalo horns. Beyond wood and ivory, *netsuke* craftsmen gave polish to a wide array of materials: lacquerware with gold or silver *maki-e* (p. 108) touches in addition to mother-of-pearl inlays; metals such as gold, silver, and *shakudo* (p. 109); ceramics in the name of Hirado and Raku ware, as well as coral, claws from birds of prey, cloisonné (p. 109), and plant seeds.

Motifs emerged from just about anything, from animals, including mythical dragons and phoenixes, to fruits and vegetables, flowers and other types of plant life, to trade tools, the *netsuke* owner's family crest, theater, occupations, seasonal events, and legends.

根付の材質と図柄

　もっとも多く使われている根付の材料は木と象牙で、木の種類ではツゲがもっとも多い。象牙は輸入品のため高価な材料ではあるが、細かい細工ができるので好んで用いられた。牙では、セイウチや猪の牙も用いられ、鹿や水牛の角なども用いられた。そのほか、蒔絵 (p.108) や螺鈿などの漆製品、金・銀・赤銅 (p.109) などの金属、平戸焼や楽焼などの陶磁器、珊瑚、猛禽の爪、七宝 (p.109)、植物の種など多種多様な素材が使用されている。

　根付の図柄は動物、龍や鳳凰などの想像上の動物、野菜や果物、花や植物、さまざまな道具、持ち主の家紋、芸能、職業、四季の行事、故事伝説など、ありとあらゆるものが表されているといってもいい。

Ivory Ring *Netsuke*
Edo Period

An early version *wanuke*, or pull-ring type *netsuke*, practical in looping together numerous *sagemono*, such as flint bags and hollowed out gourds used as sake flasks. Conceivably dating back to the early Edo period. The high-grade ivory implies it may have belonged to a samurai family. Though relatively rare today, its simple design detracts from making it viable to *netsuke* collectors.

象牙輪抜け根付　江戸時代
　「輪抜け」という、輪状の根付。燧袋や瓢箪などいくつもの提物を吊ることのできる実用的な根付で、根付の初期の形式。制作時期は江戸前期にさかのぼると思われる。高級な象牙を使っていることから、武家の持ち物だろう。デザインとしては単純なので、根付の収集家にあまり人気がないが、現存品は多くない。

Ivory Dog *Netsuke*
Edo Period

Here, a *netsuke* dog of Western breed, coupled with a Dutch chintz tobacco pouch, hint at a fascination for things foreign. Among the animals that figure prominently in the *netsuke* scheme are the twelve animals of the zodiac, one of them being the dog. Conceivably, the dog depicted here was commissioned by someone born in the year of the dog.

象牙犬根付　江戸時代

　オランダ更紗でつくられたたばこ入れに付属した根付で、犬は洋犬であらわされており、舶来趣味の取り合わせといえる。動物の図柄のなかでも十二支は作例が多く、この作品は戌年生まれの持ち主の注文かもしれない。

Hawk's Claw *Netsuke*
Edo Period

A hawk's claw, shaped while soft, then dried. To *bubaru*, or arm oneself with a steely look and courageous action appealed to the sense of masculinity. The use of claws of beasts such as bears, wolves and birds of prey as *netsuke* also characterized such an aspect. This *netsuke* attached to a flint bag was likely the property of a samurai family.

鷹の爪根付　江戸時代

　鷹の爪をやわらかいうちに形をととのえ、乾燥させたもの。いかめしい顔をしたり、勇ましそうにふるまったりして、男の強さをアピールすることを「武張る」といい、猛禽や狼、熊など勇猛な動物の爪を根付にすることも「武張る」うちのひとつであった。燧袋に付属した根付で、おそらく武家の持ち物だろう。

Coral *Netsuke*
Edo Period

A playful vignette of a crab fashioned from deer horn, cupped in a piece of red coral, matched with a mermaid-print flint bag. The coral seen here was presumably imported as coral harvesting in Japanese waters did not begin until the Meiji period. This item is thought to have belonged to an upper-class samurai family.

珊瑚根付　江戸時代

　赤珊瑚に鹿の角でつくった蟹を添えた、遊び心のある意匠が見どころ。人魚を図柄にした燧袋に付属したもので、珊瑚は人魚との取り合わせということがわかる。日本の海で珊瑚漁が始まったのは明治時代からで、江戸時代の珊瑚は舶来品。上流の武家の持ち物と思われる。

Fishing Scene on Seed *Netsuke*
Edo Period

A fisherman steers his boat with his octopus catch on one side of a large seed (of unknown fruit). Meanwhile on the other side of the seed, a fisherman, his catch, and his net basket etch another part of the narrative. The glass *ojime* (p. 109) of the accompanying flint bag cleverly ties in with the maritime theme.

種彫漁猟図根付　江戸時代

　大きな果実の種（果実は不明）を舟に見立て、舵取りをする漁師と大きな蛸を線刻している。裏も同じく漁師と魚、網籠などを彫っている。燧袋に付属した根付で、緒締（p.109）のガラスとうまく取り合わせている。

Rosewood Ashtray *Netsuke*
Edo Period

A flint tool kit, consisting in part of a small bag of tinder (left), such as mugwort, connected to a piece of fire steel with a length of cord. To use: Place the tinder in the dish-shaped rosewood *netsuke*. Ignite the tinder with a flint. Blow on it till the sparks glow, then transfer the flame. Once the user's *kiseru* is lit, the *netsuke* turns into an ashtray. Flint, steel, and tinder, all in an easy to-go pouch (right).

紫檀灰落とし根付　江戸時代

　火打道具の一式。鋼鉄片の火打金と紐で結ばれている小袋（左）の中に火口と呼ばれる燃料（もぐさなど）が入っている。火口を紫檀でつくった皿状の根付に置き、火打石で点火し、息を吹いて火を大きくして他のものに火を移す。根付はきせるの灰皿でもあるので、「灰落とし」の名がある。いずれの道具も巾着（右）に入れて携帯する。

Hirado Ware *Netsuke* with *Unryu* Motif
Edo Period

In early Edo, the warrior class popularized the trend of *aisage*, or hanging two objects, an *inro* with a *kinchaku*, from their waist. The porcelain of this *netsuke* is of the Hirado ware type, a white porcelain developed in Nagasaki prefecture, and is decorated with an *unryu* motif. The *hyaku-hida* (lit. hundred-fold) leather *kinchaku* carried flint.

平戸焼雲龍図根付　江戸時代

　江戸の初期に武士の間で印籠を提げる風習が起こり、印籠と巾着を一緒に提げる「合提げ」という形式が流行する。根付の平戸焼は長崎県で生産される白磁で、雲龍の絵が染付けされている。巾着は革製で、襞の多い「百襞巾着」と呼ばれる形式。巾着の中には火打石を入れる。

Gourd Shaped Copper *Netsuke*
Late Edo to Meiji Period

A velvet drawstring *nioi-bukuro* coupled with a paulownia *inro*, belonging to a woman, probably a geisha. The scent of incense exudes from the *nioi-bukuro*, which is used as a sachet. The toggle, a gourd-shaped *netsuke* with a screw-on lid, stores tiny pills.

瓢箪型銅製根付　幕末〜明治時代
　ビロードでつくった匂い袋と桐製の印籠の合提げ。女物で、おそらく芸者の持ち物だろう。香を入れた匂い袋からは、布を通して匂いが染み出てくる。根付の瓢箪は、口の蓋がねじ式で開閉でき、中に小さな丸薬などを入れることができる。

Chapter 3

Fukuromono

第三章

袋物

History of *Fukuromono*

Fukuromono is a general term employed to describe bag-shaped containers. *Fukuromono* are used to collect, carry, store or organize items. The history of *fukuromono* in Japan dates back to prehistoric times, with woven bark-fiber bags discovered among the artifacts of the Jomon period (ca. 10,000-300 BCE). Most common throughout the ancient and medieval periods were *hiuchi-bukuro*, or flint bags that held fire-starters, *kinchaku*, or drawstring pouches hanging from the waist, and *uwazashi-bukuro* bags large enough to transport clothes and tools. The Momoyama period (1568-1600) saw rare and imported fabrics such as wool and velvet fashioned into bags. During the Edo period, when *tenka taihei* (lit. great peace) reigned over the land, a rich and luxurious culture began to blossom for the warrior and merchant classes. This upscaled lifestyle brought popularity to *fukuromono*, both as necessities and as fashion accessories.

袋物の歴史

　袋物とは袋の形をした物入れの総称。物を袋の中に収めたり、携行したり、保存、整理するのに用いられる。日本における袋物の歴史は有史以前にさかのぼり、縄文時代の遺跡から、樹皮で編んだ袋が発見されている。古代・中世を通して最も多く用いられた袋物は、火打石などを入れた「燧袋」や「巾着」など腰間から提げたものと、衣類や道具などを入れる「上刺し袋」という大きな袋だった。桃山時代には羅紗やビロードなどの珍奇な素材が輸入され、袋物にも利用されるようになる。そして天下泰平の江戸時代になり、武家や商人を中心に絢爛奢侈な文化が花開くと、袋物は必需品として、またファッションアクセサリーとしてもてはやされるようになった。

Types of *Fukuromono*

Before the Edo period, money was carried in flint bags or drawstring pouches, but with the onset of the Edo period *kami-ire*, or paper holders, also began serving as wallets and designs took on an air of sophistication.

Tobacco pouches came onto the scene during the Edo period when, thanks to the cultivation of tobacco in Japan, smoking became a popular pastime.

No less elegant were the women's pouches, which ranged from *nioi-bukuro*, or incense sachets, and portable mirror cases designed to be tucked into the front of a kimono to *hakoseko*, or cosmetic cases.

袋物の種類

　江戸時代以前は燧袋や巾着に貨幣を入れていたが、江戸時代になると巾着のほかに「紙入れ」も財布として使われるようになり、豪華な紙入れがつくられるようになる。

　江戸時代初期に国内でたばこが栽培されるようになると喫煙の習慣が広まり、巾着にたばこを入れて携帯するようになり、袋物のたばこ入れが誕生する。

　女性の袋物は、香を入れる「匂い袋」、携帯用の鏡を入れる「懐中鏡入れ」や化粧道具入れの「筥迫」など、奢侈な風潮にともなって華やかな袋物がつくられるようになった。

European Chintz *Kami-ire*
Edo Period

A copperplate-printed chintz *kami-ire*. The sailing ship and person depicted on the fabric are believed to be based on a story of Western origin. The clasps on the case consist of *shakudo* inlays of a Dutchman and a Western dog. This was very likely a custom order for a wealthy person with a taste for imported goods.

木綿ヨーロッパ更紗紙入れ　江戸時代

　木綿地に銅板で模様を染め付けた更紗の紙入れ。絵柄は帆船と人物で、西洋の物語に題材をとったものと思われる。前金具は赤銅色絵打出し彫りのオランダ人と洋犬図。舶来好みの富裕層が特注したものだろう。

Indigo *Kami-ire* with *Karako* Motif
Edo Period

A *kami-ire* with the *karako*, or Chinese children, motif embroidered on indigo-dyed silk. The figure of a foreigner is carved on the thin brass clasp. The foreign figure theme is taken from *shunga*, or erotic art. Courtesans visited Dejima Island (p. 110) in Nagasaki Harbor at the request of their Dutch customers and these scenes were depicted in *shunga* art.

藍唐子文織紙入れ　江戸時代

　藍染の絹地に唐子模様を織り出している唐様の紙入れ。前金具は真鍮薄肉彫りの異人図。この異人図は春画から題材をとったもの。長崎では遊女がオランダ人の求めに応じて出島（p.110）に出向くことが行われ、その様子が春画の題材となった。

Angel Motif on Dutch *Kinkarakawa Kami-ire*
Edo Period

A two-fold gold-leafed *kinkarakawa* (p. 110) *kami-ire* representative of the Dutch Baroque era. The case opens up to show an outstretched angel on the inside holding a peacock feather in its right hand. When closed, the case is secured by a flat chain fitted with the silver *shakudo* carving of a phoenix.

オランダ金唐革人形手紙入れ　江戸時代

　オランダ・バロック時代の金唐革 (p.110) で、ふたつ折りの紙入れ。展開すると、紙入れいっぱいにエンジェルが描かれ、その右手には孔雀の羽を持っている。紙入れを巻く胴締は板鎖で、掛金具は銀赤銅打出し彫りの鳳凰文。

Chirashi Embroidered European Chintz *Kami-ire*
Edo Period

A *kami-ire* of European chintz showing four soldiers on the front flap and a sailing ship on the back, embroidered in *chirashi,* a running stitch technique that outlines the curves pictured on the fabric. A Dutch East India Company (VOC) coin, minted in silver and featuring a sailing ship, accents the flap. A *kami-ire* rich with fascination of the Dutch.

木綿ヨーロッパ散縫更紗紙入れ　江戸時代

　表に4人の兵士、裏に帆船を描いたヨーロッパ更紗に、輪郭を強調する散縫という縫い方を施している。前金具は帆船が描かれたオランダ東インド会社の銀貨を用いている。オランダ趣味がよく出ている紙入れといえよう。

Large *Kami-ire* with *Sagara* Embroidery
Edo Period

This large *kami-ire* showcases the ultimate in *sagara* embroidery (a knotting technique). The flat chain boasts an exquisite arrangement of fine gold inlay on *shakudo* and the outer covering is of Dutch velvet. The scene on the *kami-ire* depicts the legendary 10th-century warlord Tawara Tota being empowered by the dragon god living on Chikubu Island in Lake Biwa, Shiga prefecture before going to slay the giant centipede. The dragon god appears on the front, and Tawara Tota, on the back.

相良縫大型紙入れ　江戸時代

　大型の紙入れで、相良縫いの極致を示す作品。板鎖は赤銅地に細かい金の布目象嵌が施されたもので、豪華な取り合わせ。外入れはオランダのビロード。紙入れの絵柄は、武将の俵藤太がムカデ退治に向かう際に、琵琶湖の竹生島（滋賀県）に棲む龍神から力を与えられる場面。表に龍神、裏に俵藤太を表している。

Kaishi-ire with Cutouts on Crepe Fabric

Edo Period

A dedicated container for *kaishi* (p. 111) paper. An *osaiku-mono*, or handcraft adopted by daughters of upper-class samurai families and palace maids as a form of enjoyment. The cutouts are attached to a crepe fabric backing using a technique similar to appliqué called *kiribame* (p. 111). Plum blossoms decorate the front, while Japanese irises adorn the back. A silver sachet hangs from the flat-knit closure strap.

縮緬切嵌懐紙入れ　江戸時代

　懐紙 (p.111) だけを入れる紙入れ。上流の武家の娘や御殿女中が手慰みにつくった「お細工物」の一種。縮緬に切嵌 (p.111) というアップリケに似た技法で模様を付けている。表は梅、裏は菖蒲の絵柄。胴締は平打ちの紐で、銀製の巾着型の匂い袋を付ける。

Gozabune Shaped *Kami-ire*

Edo Period

Although looking like a regular *kami-ire* inside and out, once opened, it resembles a *gozabune*, or a ship reserved for the nobles. Not for practical purposes, but crafted more as an *osaiku-mono* by palace maids. Their creativity was used to repurpose scraps of silk or wool into ships or Girls' Day decorations and other items in the style of *oshi-e* (p. 111). Very few pieces remain today, making these valuable Edo artifacts.

御座船型御細工物紙入れ　江戸時代

　表面も内側も普通の紙入れと同じつくりだが、中を開くと組み立て式の御座船になる。これは実用品ではなく、御殿女中などが手慰みにつくったお細工物の一種。お女中同士で図案を考え、錦や羅紗などの端切れを押絵（p.111）風に貼り付け、船や雛

上／閉じたところ。
下／閉じたところから展開してゆく途中。

Kami-ire shown here when closed.

Kami-ire in the process of being opened.

壇などがつくられた。完成品で残っているものは非常に少なく、貴重な江戸の文物といえよう。

Tsuzure-ori Fabric *Tabako-ire*
Edo Period

The most popular type of *tabako-ire* consisted of two parts, a long case for the *kiseru* pipe and a *kamasu* pouch for the finely-cut tobacco. Here, the two sections are connected by an *ojime* clamp. Stylized waves decorate the *tsuzure-ori* (p. 112). The *kamasu* pouch is held fast by a metal carp. The flap, when opened, echoes the carp motif on the inside. The silver *ojime* clamp consists of three moveable parts reminiscent of waves washing over coral.

綴れ織筒提げたばこ入れ　江戸時代

　筒提げたばこ入れはもっともポピュラーな形態で、きせるを収納する筒とたばこを入れる「叺」、筒と叺をつなぐ緒締で構成される。叺は綴れ織 (p.112) で波の柄を表し、鯉の鉄製の前金具を付ける。叺の被 (蓋) を開けると鯉の絵柄が現れるという趣向。緒締は銀で波を表し珊瑚をあしらう。3段で構成され、蝶番で動くようになっている。

Tabako-ire Set Embroidered with Autumnal Insects
Edo Period

A *tabako-ire* used by the wife of a high-ranking samurai. The *kiseru* case and *kamasu* are of rare dark green wool. The bamboo grass is embroidered in gold thread while the dragonflies are outlined in black. Nesting among the *shakudo* branches and leaves are persimmons shaped from orange coral. The chain linking the *kiseru* case and *kamasu* alludes to the famed Tatsutagawa River in Nara prefecture, its autumn leaves bobbing past the crescent moon reflected on the water.

ふかみどり
深緑羅紗地秋虫図刺繍筒提げたばこ入れ　江戸時代

　身分の高い武家の奥方が使用した筒提げたばこ入れ。筒と叺は、非常に珍しい深緑色の羅紗で仕立てられ、それぞれに笹を金糸で、トンボを黒糸で刺繍している。前金具は赤銅打出し彫りで柿の枝葉をつくり、実は珊瑚を嵌め込んでいる。筒と叺を繋ぐ鎖部分は、流水に浮かぶ紅葉と川面に映る三日月で立田川（奈良県）を表す。

Yagasuri Pattern on Velvet Mirror Case
Edo Period

Geometric shaped *yagasuri* arrow feathers woven into Japanese velvet. The arrow is considered a symbol of good luck, since once shot with a bow, it never returns. For this reason, the arrow motif was incorporated at times into a marriageable girl's kimono or accessories as part of her trousseau. This mirror case probably belonged to the daughter of a prominent samurai family.

矢絣柄ビロード懐中鏡入れ　江戸時代

　図案化した矢羽根が連続する模様の矢絣柄を、日本製のビロードで織り出している。弓で射た矢は戻ってこないことから、縁起物として嫁入りの際に矢絣柄の着物や小物を用意することがあった。この懐中鏡入れは、上流の武家の娘の持ち物だろう。

The case holds a small mirror and a pill case. The mirror, having been made of imported glass and mercury, has blackened over the years. The long *kogai* and *kanzashi* hair ornaments belonged to the same owner of the case, and are made of silver. Sliding off the bellflower decoration will turn it into a pair of chopsticks. The *kogai* on the far left is made of the leg bone of a crane.

中身は懐中鏡と丸薬いれの小箱。鏡は舶来ガラス製で水銀を用いているため年月が経つと劣化して黒くなってしまう。笄と簪は、懐中鏡入れと同じ持ち主のもので、銀製と鶴の脛骨製。銀製の簪は、桔梗の飾りをスライドして外すと箸になる。

Mirror Case with Gold *Aoi-mon*

Edo Period

Large and small *aoi-mon* (hollyhock family crests), brocaded in gold against the diagonal latticework, give this mirror case a sense of subtle refinement. The case opens up to a poem accredited to Tokugawa Nariaki (1800-60), former feudal lord of the Mito domain. Inked in gold on a wine-colored background, this item was possibly endowed as a reward.

葵紋金襴懐中鏡入れ　江戸時代

　斜めの格子に大小の葵紋を金襴で織り出した品格ある懐中鏡入れ。中を開けると牡丹臙脂の内貼りに、水戸藩主・徳川斉昭直筆の歌が金泥で認められている。おそらく恩賞用に下げ渡されたものと思われる。

The poem reads, "My dear friend, despite my promise to keep the mirror clear of fog, fog fills my heart each time I dream." — Tokugawa Nariaki, Junior Third Rank. Another family crest, this time the *mokko-mon*, is engraved on the outside band. This indicates that the band was a custom order for the recipient of the case. A crystal ball with a *sakura*, or cherry blossoms, motif is attached to a mirror decorated with *kiku-mon* (chrysanthemum crests).

歌は、「曇らぬと友と契らむ　ますかがみ　ゆめみるたびに　こころみが来て　従三位斉昭」と書かれている。付属の胴締は、もらい受けた人物がつくらせたもので、木瓜紋が打ち出されている。菊紋をあしらった鏡には桜を彫った水晶玉が取り付けられている。

Hakoseko with Peony Embroidery
Edo Period

A *hakoseko* lavishly embroidered with peonies and boulders on fabric woven with gilded strands of *washi* paper. The accompanying *nioi-bukuro*, resembling an *inro*, is shaped in gold plated silver. A shimmering *hakoseko-kanzashi* hairpin, with ornamental chains longer than those for regular *kanzashi*, rounds out this set. At the end of each chain is a decorative piece called *bira-bira*, in this instance peonies that accentuate the overall theme.

<ruby>金<rt>きん</rt></ruby><ruby>紙<rt>し</rt></ruby><ruby>織<rt>おり</rt></ruby><ruby>地<rt>じ</rt></ruby>牡丹刺繍文筥迫　江戸時代

　金糸で織られた地に、岩と牡丹を刺繍した華やかな筥迫。付属の匂い袋は、銀に金鍍金を施した印籠型。筥迫に合わせてつくった「筥迫簪」がセットになっている。鎖は通常よりも長いのが特徴で、先端に「びらびら金具」と呼ばれる飾りが付く。このびらびら金具は牡丹文で、筥迫の生地の牡丹文と取り合わせている。

Hakoseko with Vertical Floral Design
Edo Period

A *hakoseko* covered in Dutch floral copperplate-printed velvet. The case is enclosed not by the usual flat chain, but by three *shakudo* chains, secured by a cloisonné clasp that highlights the flower pattern of the case. References to the *bugaku* court dance hang from the decorative chains on the side. One is a *torikabuto* (lit. bird's helmet) headpiece and the other is a *sho*, a musical reed instrument. Possibly belonging to an upper-class samurai family.

ビロード地竪花柄文銅板更紗筥迫　江戸時代

　オランダ製花柄文のビロードの筥迫。胴締は通常の板鎖ではなく、赤銅製の鎖が3本付き、掛金具には花文の七宝が華やかさを添えている。付属の華鎖は通常よりも1本多く垂れ下がり、舞楽で使用される鳥兜と笙の金具付きで、凝った取り合わせとなっている。上流の武家の持ち物だろう。

Chapter 4

Hair Ornaments

第四章

髪の装い

History of Hair Ornaments

The earliest *kushi*, or comb, found in Japan was made of wood, excavated among the artifacts of the Jomon period that date back some 7,000 years. Throughout the ages, from Jomon to premodern, *kushi* were inserted into the hair more as talismans to ward off evil rather than for the practical purpose of combing hair. But with the onset of *tenka taihei*, a time of peace and prosperity in early Edo, women began to flaunt their individuality with diverse upswept hairdos. This touched off a surging flow of new designs for *kushi*, *kogai*, and *kanzashi*. Historically, until early Edo or the mid-17th century, hair ornaments of costly material and lavish design were considered the realm of aristocratic and samurai wives. This changed, however, from mid-Edo or the mid-18th century, when the townspeople, economic clout in hand, became the bearers of culture. Innovative and elaborate hair accessories soon became the trend.

髪飾りの歴史

　　日本で最古といわれる「櫛」は、今から約7000年前の縄文時代の遺跡から出土した木製の櫛である。縄文時代から近世以前までの長い期間、櫛は髪を梳く実用面よりも、頭に挿して魔除けとする意味合いが大きかった。江戸時代になり、天下泰平の世が訪れると、女性たちはさまざまな形の髷を結んで個性を主張しはじめ、櫛のほか「笄」、「簪」などの髪飾りも急速に発展した。江戸の前期頃までは、高価な素材に贅沢な装飾を施した髪飾りは、貴族や武家階級の女性に限定されていたが、江戸中期以降は貴族や武家よりも豊かな経済力を持つ町人階級が文化の担い手となり、自由な発想でつくられた奢侈で華美な髪飾りが流行した。

Types of Accessories and Materials Used

The *kazari-kushi* was a decorative comb, which changed dramatically in material, shape, and ornamentation since the mid-Edo period. The *kogai* was initially a stick-shaped accessory, around which ladies-in-waiting who served in palaces wrapped their hair. With the arrival of the Edo period, however, the *kogai* was made to be inserted into an updo. The *kanzashi* is an elaborate hairpin that dates back to the Nara period (710-94). Among the numerous hair items crafted during the Edo period, many of them were shaped like ear picks at the top. This functional form provided a loophole from the frequent bans on opulent hair ornaments. Indeed, tortoiseshell, metal, wood, ivory, and glass were embellished with designs in lacquer, gold *maki-e* on lacquer, mother-of-pearl, gold plating, inlay, and openwork.

髪飾りの種類と素材

　髪を飾るための櫛は「飾り櫛」といい、江戸中期以降の飾り櫛は材質、形状、装飾が多彩に変化していった。笄は、もともとは宮中の女官が髪を巻き付けるための棒状のものだったが、江戸時代になると結い上げた髷の中に挿し込む形のものがつくられた。簪は奈良時代まで遡るとされる華やかな髪飾り。江戸時代にはさまざまな種類の簪がつくられたが、頭（先端）は耳かきになっているものが多い。江戸時代はたびたび贅沢な髪飾りが禁じられたので、耳かきを付けることで髪飾りではないということにしたからである。髪飾りの素材は鼈甲、金属、木、象牙、ガラスなどがあり、そこに漆、蒔絵、螺鈿、金鍍金、象嵌、透かし彫りなどの装飾が施された。

Unmottled Tortoiseshell *Kogai, Kushi* and *Kanzashi*

Late Edo to Meiji Period

Bekko (p. 112) tortoiseshell is normally yellow in color with dark brown mottling. *Shiro bekko* (lit. white tortoiseshell) was attained through a complex process of scraping off and molding only the yellow portions with heat and water into a sheet of raw material, the end product of which brought in a good price. The ensemble shown here once graced the coiffure of a marriageable girl. The *kogai* (top) and four *kanzashi*, also of *shiro bekko*, are adorned with flowers and birds.

白鼈甲の笄、櫛、簪　幕末〜明治時代
「鼈甲」(p.112) は黄色い部分と濃褐色の斑（斑点）が混在している。斑を除いて黄色い部分だけを削り、熱と水で加工して板状にしたものを「白鼈甲」といい、高値がついた。この白鼈甲でつくった髪飾り一式は婚礼用の豪華なもの。笄（上）と4本の簪の飾りは、同じく白鼈甲で花鳥を表している。

Unmottled Tortoiseshell *Maezashi*

Edo Period

As the word *mae*, or front, in the name suggests, this *maezashi* is inserted into hair that is coiled above the face. Worn by a young lady from a wealthy family, the three auspicious symbols of pine, bamboo and plum, in addition to the crane of longevity, intertwine gracefully in this work of art. Scattered spheres of red coral that accent the crane's head, for example, add color and luxe.

白鼈甲の前挿し　江戸時代

　「前挿し」は名前のとおり結った髪の前側に挿す飾り。本作品は富裕な若い女性が挿した前挿しで、白鼈甲で松竹梅に鶴を表した縁起物の細工が見事。鶴の頭部分など、各所に紅珊瑚を配して、彩りと豪華さを付している。

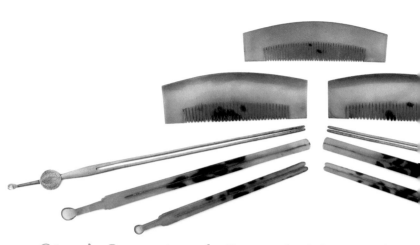

Oiran's *Sanmai-gushi* Set with Silver and Tortoiseshell *Kanzashi*

Edo Period

The accoutrements of an *oiran* (p. 112), this *sanmai-gushi*, or trio of combs, was designed to be worn as a set. *Oiran* aesthetics generally differed between the Kamigata region of Kyoto and Osaka, versus the Kanto region of Edo. Hair ornaments of Kamigata *oiran* were a rich display of opulence. *Oiran* in Edo, on the other hand, adopted an understated look. The subdued look of these accessories implies an Edo sensibility. The climbing wisteria etched on the two silver *kanzashi* suggests that this may have been the family crest of the patron who gifted this set.

花魁三枚櫛、銀簪、鼈甲簪　江戸時代

　花魁 (p.112) が用いた櫛と簪。「三枚櫛」は3枚セットで髪に挿す簪のこと。一般的に花魁の髪飾りは、上方が派手で、江戸はあっさりしている。これらの櫛や簪は派手さがないので江戸の花魁の用いた典型的な髪飾りといえる。銀の簪には「上がり藤」の紋が表されている。花魁にこれらの櫛や簪を贈った馴染み客の家紋だろう。

礒田湖龍斎筆
「雛形若菜の初模様 蔦屋内しほきぬ」
安永年間後期（1777 ～ 80）頃
三枚櫛を挿した花魁の図。

Isoda Koryusai, *Hinagata wakana no hatsu moyo*
Tsutaya-uchi Shiokinu [**New Year's Fashion as**
Worn by Tsutaya's Shiokinu], Late An'ei Era (1777-80)
Portrait of an *oiran* wearing a *sanmai-gushi* set.

Tortoiseshell *Kanzashi*
Edo Period

A composition of peonies and a fan, under which a *shaguma* (a sort of wig of yak fur dyed in red) emerges. In the noh and kabuki performances of *Shakkyo* (lit. Stone Bridge), the spirit of a lion dances in a field of peonies on a mountain. The song from the noh stage made such a hit among the warrior class that this samurai wife's *kanzashi* seems to evoke strains from the music.

Toyohara Kunichika, *Peonies* of *Shakkyo*,
Sawamura Tossho as Fuki Saburo (1867)
A scene from the kabuki play *Shakkyo*.

鼈甲箸　江戸時代

　扇と牡丹のつぼみが組み合わされ、扇の下には赤熊（赤く染めたヤクの毛）が出ている。これは能や歌舞伎の演目『石橋』で、霊獣の獅子が山一面の牡丹の中で舞う場面を表したもの。能の脚本に節をつけて歌う謡曲が武士階級にも流行したことから、武家の奥方の箸に取り入れられたのだろう。

Tortoiseshell *Kanzashi*
Edo Period

Five tortoiseshell *kanzashi*, each topped with intricate designs. From far right: two turtles, a peony with small birds, plum blossoms and a small bird, a puffy sparrow (a sparrow with rounded feathers), and a peony. The decorative tops are carved separately, then glued to the main body. The dark spots of the tortoiseshell are skillfully used as highlights on the third and fourth *kanzashi* from the right.

鼈甲簪　江戸時代

　5本の鼈甲簪。細工の図柄は右から2匹の亀、牡丹に小禽、梅に小禽、ふくら雀（羽毛が丸くふくらんだ雀）、牡丹。いずれも細工部分を別に彫って、膠で本体部分に接着している。鼈甲には斑と呼ばれる濃褐色の斑点があり、右から3本目と4本目の簪のように、斑点の部分を効果的に用いているところも見どころである。

Silver *Kanzashi*
Edo to Meiji Period

The base of all five *kanzashi* is in silver, while the three in the center are gold-plated. The ornamentation, from right, are: *minogame* (an imaginary turtle able to transform itself into a dragon), turtles on a hanging scroll, a circular sea bream, and two cranes. The crane on the far left is cast in iron, the intricate lines of its small body masterfully inlaid with gold.

銀簪　江戸時代〜明治時代

　5本とも本体が銀製の簪で、中央の3本は本体に金鍍金を施している。細工の図柄はいずれも縁起物で、右から蓑亀（龍に変身するとされる想像上の亀）、掛け軸に亀、円形にデザインされた鯛、鶴の細工2本。左端の鶴の細工部分は鉄製で、鶴の胴の部分に細かな金象嵌を施しており、見事な出来ばえである。

Bira-bira Kanzashi

Edo Period

The decorative pieces hanging from the chains are called *bira*, while the entire hairpin is called *bira-kanzashi* or *bira-bira kanzashi*. The two shown here are made of silver. The *kanzashi* on top recaptures the fable of Urashima Taro, who rode a turtle to the sea-god's palace (Ryugu-jo), and returned home with a jeweled box. The flat *kanzashi* below it is exquisitely engraved with peonies and butterflies, enhanced by dangling glitters of three-dimensional peonies.

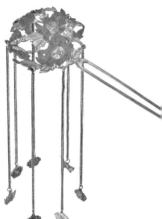

びらびら簪　江戸時代

　鎖でぶら下がった飾りを「びら」といい、びらの付いた簪を「びら簪」とか「びらびら簪」と呼ぶ。2本とも銀製。上の簪の細工部分は、浦島太郎が亀にのって龍宮城へ行き、玉手箱を得て帰ってきたという物語の見立て。下の平打簪は、牡丹と蝶を表した頭部分の彫金が見事で、びらの牡丹の飾りも立体的に仕上げられている。

All three items shown here are in silver. The hollow circle of the *kanzashi* at the top is gold-plated, while the fluttering *bira* butterflies that connect to it, add play. To note, this hollow circle design also appears on family crests.

The bottom two *kanzashi* are chrysanthemum filigrees executed in silver, with dangling *bira* chrysanthemums etched to match. The technique of twisting fine metal strands into exquisite forms was a foreign influence, introduced in Hirado Port, Nagasaki prefecture and developed locally as *Hirado-zaiku*.

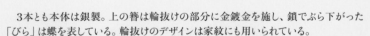

　3本とも本体は銀製。上の簪は輪抜けの部分に金鍍金を施し、鎖でぶら下がった「びら」は蝶を表している。輪抜けのデザインは家紋にも用いられている。
　下2本の細工は、銀の針金をひねって菊を表し、「びら」も菊を表している。このような針金細工の技法は舶来のもので、長崎では「平戸細工」として発展した。

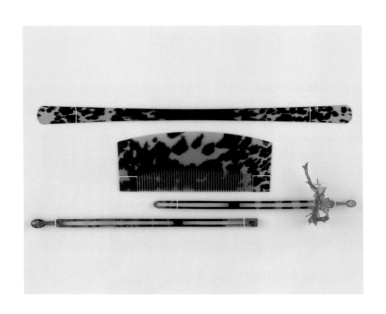

Mottled Tortoiseshell *Kogai*, *Kushi*, and *Kanzashi*
Edo Period

Tortoiseshell is known for its characteristic *balafu* spots, or mottling. While unmottled *shiro bekko* is prized, items like the ones here accentuate the mottling to their best advantage. Of the two *kanzashi* shown at the bottom, the upper one is decorated with a branch of coral, while the rod on the lower one is decorated in gold *maki-e* work.

バラ斑入り鼈甲の笄、櫛、簪　江戸時代
　バラ斑とは、まだら模様に斑が入っていること。斑の入っていない白鼈甲が珍重されるいっぽうで、本作品のようにバラ斑をうまくデザインに利用して、よい味わいを醸し出しているものもある。簪2本のうち、上の簪は飾りに枝珊瑚を用い、下の簪は脚(あし)(棒状の部分)に金蒔絵を施している。

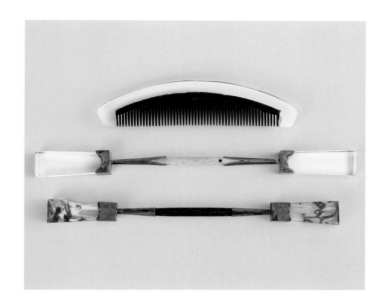

Edo Glass *Kushi* and *Kogai*
Edo Period

A summer set of accessories that evoke a sense of coolness. Probably worn by a well-to-do middle-aged woman residing in a *machiya* townhouse. Top: A comb with an Edo glass shaft and tortoiseshell teeth. Center: Edo glass is fitted at both ends of this *kogai*. The rod in the center is ivory and the joints are silver. Bottom: Copper powder embellishes the Edo glass on this *kogai*. The rod is ebony and the joints are brass.

江戸ガラス製の櫛と笄　江戸時代

　夏用の涼しげな櫛と笄のセットで、富裕な町家の中年女性が用いたものだろう。櫛の峰（持ち手部分）は江戸ガラス、歯の部分は鼈甲製。2本の笄のうち上は、左右の飾りが江戸ガラスで、脚（棒状の部分）は象牙製、金具は銀製。下の笄は、左右の飾りが銅粉を流して模様をつくった江戸ガラス、脚は黒檀製、金具は真鍮製である。

Chapter 5

Makeup Tools

第五章

化粧道具

Cosmetics of the Edo Period

Makeup for women of this period consisted fundamentally of white *oshiroi* face powder, red *beni* for the lips, and black *mayuzumi* for the eyebrows, as well as a teeth blackener called *ohaguro* (p. 113). That said, social status and norms held sway even in these areas of grooming. Women generally blackened their teeth upon marriage and shaved their eyebrows at the sign of pregnancy. Teeth blackening, however, ended during the Meiji period when foreigners new to the country expressed their shock. Aristocratic women were the first to discontinue the practice, followed gradually by women of the general public. But it was face powder that preoccupied women the most. Fair skin was a sign of youth and proof of their upper echelon status that dispensed with having to labor under the burning sun. The shade of lip color also trended with the times. When a government edict banned luxurious hair ornaments, the crimson color of the *beni* took on a lighter hue.

江戸時代の化粧

　江戸時代の女性たちの化粧は白粉をつけ、唇に紅をさし、眉を描き、歯を黒く染める「お歯黒」(p.113) が基本だった。とはいえ、身分やさまざまな社会規範が化粧にも影響した。たとえばお歯黒は一般的には既婚者がするもので、妊娠すると眉を剃った。お歯黒は明治になると外国人に奇異な目で見られ、上流階級の女性たちがまずお歯黒をやめ、徐々に一般女性たちもしなくなった。女性たちがもっとも気をつかっていたのは白粉化粧である。色白は若さの象徴であり、日焼けをするような労働をしない上流階級であることの証でもあった。紅の濃淡も時代によって流行があり、奢侈禁止令で豪華な髪飾りが禁じられると、それに合わせて紅も薄くなる傾向があった。

Types of Makeup Tools

The two types of face powder that existed during this time were either lead-, or mercury-based. Whichever the type, the powder was mixed in a bowl with an amount of water and applied with a brush. *Beni*, extracted mainly from safflower, was sold with the red pigment brushed inside small porcelain dishes and cups, ready for use. Women shaved off their eyebrows and painted on new ones with *mayuzumi* derived from black wheat fungus and soot from burning oil. These grooming essentials, including mirrors, were gathered in a vanity box called *kesho-bako*. And for affluent women on the go, easy to carry makeup kits were indispensable. Women blackened their teeth by alternately applying powdered plant galls and a liquid called *ohaguro* water to their teeth. The regimen required its own set of *ohaguro* tools, including vessels for the liquids and a gargling bowl.

化粧道具の種類

　江戸時代の白粉は鉛でつくられた鉛白粉と水銀でつくられた軽粉の2種類があり、容器に白粉を入れて水でのばし、刷毛を使ってのばした。紅はおもに紅花からつくられたもので、皿や猪口に塗られたものが市販された。眉を剃るのは剃刀で、麦の黒穂や油煙などを使った「眉墨」で眉を描いた。これらの化粧道具や鏡を収納したのが「化粧箱」である。また、外出先で化粧するための懐中化粧道具も富裕な女性たちには必携のものだった。お歯黒は、五倍子（ヌルデの木にできた虫こぶ）を砕いた粉と、「お歯黒水」という液体を交互に歯に塗ると黒く染まった。お歯黒をする際には、これらの液を入れる壺やうがいをするための碗など、「お歯黒道具」一式を用いた。

Beni-choko

Edo Period

Cups and bowls such as these, coated on the inside with refined *beni* pigment, were called *beni-choko* or *beni-zara*. Among them are vessels produced solely to hold *beni*, while others were repurposed tableware.

紅猪口　江戸時代

　化粧用に精製された紅を塗り付ける容器。内面に紅が刷かれた小碗や小皿を「紅猪口」や「紅皿」と呼ぶ。紅猪口には、はじめから紅専用としてつくられたものや、食器などを転用したものなどさまざまある。

渓斎英泉筆「今様美人拾二景　てごわそう」
文政5〜6年（1822〜23）
左手に紅猪口、右手に紅筆を持って紅を付ける遊
女を描く。町人文化が最盛期を迎えた文化文政
期には、この絵の遊女の下唇のように、紅を濃く
付けて玉虫色に見せる「笹色紅」が流行した。

Keisai Eisen, *Imayo bijin juni-kei tegowa-so*
[Woman of Unyielding Appearance, from the
series Twelve Views of Modern Beauties], (1822-23)
A courtesan holds a *beni-choko* in her left hand while
painting her lips with her right. During the Bunka-
Bunsei era, when urban culture reached its peak, *sasa-
iro beni*, an iridescent green, was a popular color for
the lower lip.

Set of *Ohaguro* Tools
Edo Period

The largest object here is a *mimi-darai*, or ear basin, named after its *mimi*, or earlike handles. On top of the basin is a long thin tray, lined up on which are a kettle, a metal bowl, a container of powdered plant galls, and a feather brush. Below, from right to left are a jug for the *ohaguro* water, a box of plant gall, and a gargle bowl. To blacken the teeth: Boil only the requisite amount of *ohaguro* water in the kettle, pour that into the bowl, and apply it alternately with the plant gall powder to the teeth. Use the ceramic bowl to gargle. Then spit into the basin.

お歯黒道具一式　江戸時代

　中央は「耳盥」。盥に渡された板状の「渡し金」の上に「鉄漿沸」、「鉄漿坏」、五倍子粉入れ、鳥の羽でつくった刷毛が並ぶ。画面右からお歯黒水を入れる「お歯黒壺」、「五倍子箱」、「嗽茶碗」。お歯黒水を使う分だけ鉄漿沸で沸かして鉄漿坏に入れ、五倍子粉と交互に歯に塗ってゆく。嗽茶碗でうがいをし、耳盥に吐き出す。

Utagawa Kuniyoshi, *Tatoe-gusa oshie hayabiki ha*
[Teeth, from the series Index of Representative Proverbs],
(1843-47)

The first time a woman blackens her teeth before her
wedding is called *hatsukane*. Here, with her blackening tools
spread out before her, the bride-to-be checks the result of
her first ever work with her *e-kagami*, a handled mirror.

Hand Mirrors
Edo Period

The timeless design of these portable mirrors may be around even today. Since bronze mirrors were mass produced, hand mirrors of the type were used by a wide range of women, including geisha and urban dwellers. The tendency for these mirrors to cloud over time gave livelihood to itinerant mirror polishers, who revived the shine with pomegranate juice.

手鏡　江戸時代

　携帯用の鏡で、現在もこれに似たデザインの手鏡を見かけることがあるだろう。銅製の鏡は大量生産していたため、このような手鏡は芸者や町家の女性など、幅広い層の女性たちが使っていた。銅の鏡は年月が経つと曇ってくるため、ザクロの汁で曇りを除去する商売もあった。

豊原国周筆「当勢三十二想　はつかし想」
明治2年（1869）
画面右下にお歯黒道具が描かれていることから、
既婚者の証であるお歯黒をし、恥じらいながら手
鏡で染まり具合を見ている姿であろう。

Toyohara Kunichika, *Tosei sanjuni-so hazukashi-so*
[Looking Embarrassed, from the series Thirty-two
Fashionable Physiognomies], (1869)
Surmising from the teeth blackening tools at the bottom
right, the woman is married and is shyly checking her
attempt in the mirror.

Portable Cosmetic Kit
Edo Period

Touch-up essentials for the woman on the go. Unfolded, the paper mat in scattered gold leaf displays a set of face whitening utensils. To its left are two fabric cases, the smaller one for *yoji* toothpicks, the larger one to hold a *beni* palette. A bronze mirror rests in the insert of the case above. Judging from the gourd-shaped gold and *shakudo* clasp and the intricately worked chain, this case may have been owned by the wife of a wealthy merchant.

Cosmetic Kit's Decorative Chain

This triple strand *azuki* chain displays the painstaking technique of connecting tiny *azuki*, or bean-shaped links, to each other. The woven gourd at the end of the chain adds another intricate touch. Its screw-on lid suggests that the gourd may have been used to carry around tiny round pills.

懐中化粧道具　江戸時代

　携帯用の化粧道具入れの中味。金箔を散らした畳紙 (畳んで使う紙) に白粉道具一式が入っている。布製の小さな包みは、右が楊枝入れ、左が紅板 (携帯用の紅入れ)。上の化粧道具入れには銅製の鏡が挿し込んである。金鍍金と赤銅で色分けした瓢箪形の留め金や、手の込んだ華鎖などの粋な意匠からみて、富裕な商家の女性の持ち物だろう。

Unubore Mirror
Late Edo Period

Biidoro (p. 113) glass mirrors like the ones in this small *kesho-bako* were nicknamed *unubore,* or haughty, due to their high-end fabrication being reserved to a privileged few, in contrast to their common bronze counterparts. *Biidoro* mirrors entailed the exclusive use of imported sheet glass, since none was produced domestically during this period. Over time, the mercury coating on the backside of the mirrors deteriorated and rendered them unusable. Perfume vials are on the right.

うぬぼれ鏡　江戸時代後期

　ビードロ（p.113）製の鏡を使った化粧小箱。江戸時代、ガラス板は国産されてなく、すべて舶来だった。鏡は銅製が一般的で、ビードロ鏡は、他人よりも上等なものをうぬぼれて使うということから「うぬぼれ鏡」の俗称がある。ビードロ鏡は裏側に水銀を塗るため、年月が経つと劣化して使えなくなる。右側の小瓶は香水入れ。

Kesho-bako with Glass Painting
Edo Period

A portable *kesho-bako* with a reverse glass painting on the lid. *Garasu-e*, or reverse painting on glass is a technique that entails applying mud paint or oil paint, in reverse painting order, to a transparent piece of glass to be viewed from the other side. In the case shown are a mirror and a *yoji* toothpick holder. Below, from right to left are rounded pillboxes, portable *beni* palettes, brushes, a lip brush, a *beni-choko*, and a hand mirror.

ガラス絵化粧箱　江戸時代
　上蓋に「ガラス絵」が嵌められている携帯用の化粧箱。ガラス絵は透明なガラスの裏側に泥絵の具や油絵の具で絵を描いて、反対側から見る絵画技法のことで、通常の絵画とは描いてゆく順番も逆になる。箱に入っているのは鏡と楊枝入れ。画面右側から丸薬入れ、紅板、刷毛、紅用の筆、紅猪口、手鏡など。

Vanity Box with Mirror
Edo to Meiji Period

All mirrors and makeup tools were normally stored in the drawers. Here, a hole on top of the vanity accommodates a mirror stand. Cosmetic bowls and combs surround the mirror. Gargling bowls and a toothbrush made of pounded willow twigs sit on the tray next to the box. The long wooden box behind the tray holds toothbrushes and salt used as toothpaste.

Toyohara Kunichika, *Tosei sanjuni-so utsukushi-so* [Looking Beautiful, from the series Thirty-two Fashionable Physiognomies], (1869)

A woman applies *oshiroi* face powder as she peers into the mirror, her packet of powder leaning on the mirror stand.

箱型鏡台　江戸時代〜明治時代

　ふだんは鏡や化粧道具は引き出しにすべて収納されている。天板に孔が開いており、そこに鏡立てを取り付けてから鏡を掛けて使う。天板の上には紅猪口、白粉入れ、梳き櫛などが並べられている。盆の上は、嗽茶碗や房楊枝（柳の枝を叩いてつくった歯ブラシ）など。盆の上方の木箱は、房楊枝と塩（歯磨き粉の役割）を入れる。

Chapter **6**

Smoking
Utensils

第六章

喫煙道具

Smoking Culture of the Edo Period

Tobacco is believed to have been introduced to Japan toward the late 16th century by *nanban* traders (p. 114) from European countries. From the smoking bans that were issued at the onset of the Edo period, we can surmise that by then, smoking had become a popular pastime. Farmers shifted from growing rice to tobacco when leaf tobacco brought in a good market price even as a medicinal herb. To curb the trend, the shogunate frequently cracked down on tobacco, inclusive of smoking, buying, selling, and growing.

But when that proved unstoppable, the government eventually authorized the consumption of tobacco and even encouraged its cultivation. Women also took up the habit from mid-Edo onward. And as women of all social classes began relishing this new culture, smoking accoutrements evolved concurrently in numerous ways.

江戸時代の喫煙文化

　日本にたばこが西洋から伝えられた時期は、南蛮貿易 (p.114) を通じて16世紀末頃と推察される。江戸時代に入ると、早くも禁煙令が出されていることから、当時の日本人の間に、喫煙が新しい嗜好として急速に広まったことがうかがえる。当初、たばこの葉は薬としても高値がついたため、農民たちは米のかわりにたばこを栽培しはじめ、幕府はしばしばたばこの喫煙、売買、栽培を取り締まった。

　しかし、喫煙の広がりを止めることはできず、やがて喫煙は公に認められ、栽培も奨励されるようになった。江戸中期以降は女性の喫煙も一般的なものになり、社会の各層の女性たちが喫煙を楽しみ、喫煙のための道具も多彩に変化していった。

Types of Smoking Utensils

The introduction of tobacco in Japan prompted the creation of the *kiseru* pipe. The *kiseru* itself consists of a number of parts: a thimble-like pipe bowl or *hizara,* packed with a pinch of shredded tobacco; the *gankubi* (lit. gooseneck), so named because of its shape, to support the pipe bowl; the *suikuchi* or mouthpiece held in the mouth to smoke, and the *rau,* a long, tubular shaft attached to the gooseneck on one end and the mouthpiece on the other.

As urbanism settled into the late Edo period, intricate engravings began to embellish the *gankubi* and *suikuchi*. *Kiseru* produced in unconventional shapes, sometimes made entirely of metal or glass, also entered the scene. Luxurious *tabako-bon,* or tobacco trays, and *tabako-ire,* or tobacco pouches, not only kept the smoking tools handy, they reflected the tastes of the rich and well-placed.

喫煙道具の種類

　日本にたばこが伝来すると、それを吸う道具として生まれたのが「きせる」である。きせるの各部名称は、刻みたばこを詰めるところを「火皿」といい、火皿を支える部分は雁の首に似ていることから「雁首」という。口を付けてたばこを吸う部分を「吸口」といい、雁首と吸口をつなぐ管を「羅宇」という。

　江戸後期、町人文化の隆盛にともなってきせるの雁首や吸口などに彫金などの装飾が加えられ、奇抜な形のきせるが登場し、きせる全体が金属やガラスでつくられることもあった。また、喫煙道具をひとまとめにした「たばこ盆」や携帯用の「たばこ入れ」も、上流階級や富裕層の嗜好を反映して、豪華で凝った意匠のものがつくられるようになった。

Oval *Tabako-bon*

Edo Period

An oval tray resembling the large circular tub used by fishmongers to carry fish. The tray holds a *tabako-ire* drawer for shredded tobacco leaves, an *hai-otoshi* urn (center) for spent ashes, and a *hi-ire* dish for hot embers to light the *kiseru*. Vermilion is the color mainly indicative of the pleasure quarters.

<ruby>盤台形<rt>ばんだいがた</rt></ruby>たばこ盆　江戸時代

　盤台（魚屋が魚を運ぶのに用いる円形の大きな<ruby>盥<rt>たらい</rt></ruby>）を模したことが名の由来。盆の中は、きざみたばこを入れる「たばこ入れ」、灰を落とすための「灰落とし」（中央）、火種を入れる「火入れ」。本作品のように道具が朱色で統一されているものは、たいていは花柳界や花街で使われたものである。

紅の
高ご
や猫
ろ
ひ
る之を

あやにや

Suzuki Harunobu, _Seiro bijin awase_ (1770)
A courtesan takes a puff from a _shu-rau_ (a _kiseru_
with a vermilion _rau_), her single handle _tabako-bon_
in front of her.

Tabako-bon with Handle
Edo Period

A *tabako-bon* designed to be easily picked up, its red color suggestive of the pleasure quarters. The smoker would light up at the *hi-ire* on top, and after a few puffs, knock the residue from their *kiseru* into the *hai-otoshi* below. The drawers were filled with finely shredded tobacco and smoking accoutrements. The indentations on the sides serve as *kiseru* racks.

手付きたばこ盆　江戸時代

　手付きたばこ盆は、持ち運びに便利なように持ち手が付いたもの。朱塗りであることから遊郭で使われたものだろう。上の部分が火入れ、右下が灰落とし、引き出しにきざみたばこや小物を入れる。前後の両面に、きせるを掛け渡すためのくぼみがこしらえてある。

Tabako-bon with Handle
Edo Period

Whether stirred or shaken, the central *hi-ire* is designed to keep its balance thanks to its stabilizing vertical and horizontal rings. An excellent feature for the *chokibune*, a long, flat, two-to-three seater river boat used to transport people from the boathouse to the Yoshiwara pleasure quarters. A hole in the front right corner of the tray and one in the diagonally opposite corner allow smokers to insert their *kiseru*.

手付きたばこ盆　江戸時代
　中央の火入れが、垂直方向と水平方向の輪で支えられ、揺れても水平を保つ構造になっている。これは、船宿から遊郭へ向かう猪牙舟という数人用の小舟の上で使われたもの。猪牙舟は早く進むので揺れやすく、このようなたばこ盆が重宝された。右手前角と対向角にきせるを立てられるよう、天板に孔が開いている。

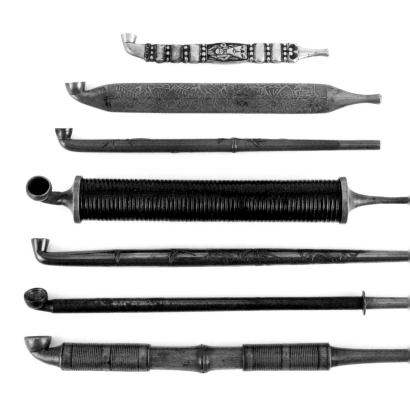

Unique Collection of *Kiseru*
Edo Period

Kiseru of varying shapes and materials. The top two are brass. The third is copper, with *gankubi* and *suikuchi* in silver. The fourth is wood, its *gankubi* and *suikuchi* in brass. The fifth is a silver *nobe-giseru*, a pipe made from a single piece of material to form the *gankubi*, *suikuchi*, and *rau*. The sixth is iron, and its *gankubi* and *suikuchi* are in brass. The seventh is bamboo with brass *gankubi* and *suikuchi*. The sixth is an early model *tsuba-tsuki kiseru*. The ring around the *suikuchi* resembles a *tsuba* (hand guard of a Japanese sword) and prevents the *kiseru* from rotating.

左ページ上から5本目の銀製きせる（左）と3本目の銅製きせる。銀製きせるは、片切彫りの技法で波に鶴の図を表している。銅製きせるは、素銅（まじりけのない銅）に銀の象嵌で竹を表している。

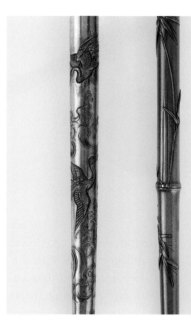

Details of the fifth silver *kiseru* and third copper *kiseru* from the previous page. The silver *kiseru* on the left features cranes flying above the waves achieved through the *katagiri-bori*, or single-cut technique. Meanwhile, the *kiseru* on the right boasts a silver inlay of bamboo on *suaka*, or refined copper.

いろいろなきせる　江戸時代

　形や材質の異なるきせる。材質は上から2本は真鍮（しんちゅう）、3本目は羅宇が銅で雁首と吸口が銀、4本目は羅宇が木製で雁首と吸口が真鍮でできている。5本目は銀製で、雁首、吸口、羅宇を1枚の延べ板でつくった「延べぎせる」である。形として古いのは6本目の「鐔付ききせる」で、鐔のような輪を吸口に付けて、きせるの回転を止める。7本目は羅宇が竹で雁首と吸口が真鍮。

Long *Kiseru*
Edo Period

A *kiseru* from the late Edo period, reminiscent of the long-stemmed *rau* of early Edo. Slung from the *obi* with the *gankubi* facing up, the *hyaku-hida kinchaku* for shredded tobacco doubled as a toggle to prevent the *kiseru* from slipping through. The *gankubi* and *suikuchi* are made of brass, silver, and refined copper. A stylish, swashbuckling look for a samurai attendant.

Tar builds up in the middle section of the *rau*. Hence, the birth of a new occupation: the *rau* vendor, who cleaned and replaced said part.

長ぎせる　江戸時代

　江戸時代前期の羅宇が長いきせるを模した江戸後期の作。雁首を上にして帯に挿して携帯した。紐で結ばれた百襞巾着がストッパーの役目を果たし、中にはきざみたばこが入っている。雁首と吸口は真鍮、銀、素銅を合わせている。奴（下僕）あた

りが、粋がって腰に挿していたものだろう。

　羅宇の中にはヤニがたまるので掃除が必要だった。かつては羅宇を掃除する「羅宇屋」という職人がたくさんいた。

Glossary

付録

用語集

Glossary | 用語集

Introduction

Tokugawa Ieyasu (1542-1616)

The first shogun of the Edo shogunate (1603-1867). Born the son of a *daimyo* in Mikawa, Aichi prefecture. At different times between the age of 6 to 19, he lived as a hostage of the nearby Oda and Imagawa warlord families. He broke his alliance with the Imagawa clan to side with Oda Nobunaga (1534-82) who unified the warriors of the Mikawa province. Ieyasu expanded his power while with Nobunaga, but submitted to Toyotomi Hideyoshi (1537-98) after Nobunaga's death. Hideyoshi's unification of Japan put the Kanto region under Ieyasu's command and gave him residence at the Edo Castle. His victory in the Battle of Sekigahara in 1600 clenched him the title of shogun. He solidified the Edo shogunate after extinguishing the Toyotomi line in 1615. Ieyasu's tomb stands on the grounds of the Nikko Toshogu Shrine in the city of Nikko, Tochigi prefecture. The crest of the Tokugawa clan is known as *mistu-aoi* (lit. three leaves of hollyhock).

徳川家康
とくがわいえやす
（1542〜1616）

江戸幕府（1603〜1867）の初代将軍。三河（愛知県）の大名の子として生まれる。6歳のときから19歳まで、織田家や今川家など近隣の大名の人質となる。今川家を離れたのちに織田信長（1534〜82）と同盟して三河を統一。信長とともに勢力を拡大するが、信長の死後に豊臣秀吉（1537〜98）に服従。秀吉の天下統一にともなって関東を領有することとなり、江戸城を居城とする。1600年の関ヶ原の戦いで、天下の主導権を握って将軍に就任。1615年に豊臣氏を滅ぼして江戸幕府を盤石のものとした。栃木県日光市の日光東照宮に墓がある。徳川一族のみが使用した葵紋は「三つ葵」という。

Daimyo

A feudal lord who retained a large number of warriors to control a vast region. A *daimyo* during the Edo period was a warrior (samurai) who received more than 10,000 *koku* of rice from the shogun — one koku being enough to feed an adult for a year. Under the *sankin kotai*, or alternate attendance system, the *daimyo* was required to lodge his wife and children in Edo, and as a rule, travel back and forth between Edo and his domain every other year. While in Edo, he was required to attend upon the shogun at Edo Castle as well as be present at the formal events held there. Some *daimyo* filled administrative positions within the shogunate.

大名 だいみょう

広大な領地を統治し、多くの家来を持つ封建領主。江戸時代は、将軍から1万石（1石は大人が1年に食べる米の量に相当する）以上の所領を与えられた武士（侍）を大名と呼んだ。江戸時代の大名は、妻子を江戸の屋敷に常駐させて、原則として1年おきに江戸と領地を行き来することが定められていた（参勤交代）。大名は江戸に滞在する期間、江戸城にいる将軍に拝謁したり、江戸城で催される儀式に参列したりすることが公務だった。また、幕府の役職につく大名もいた。

Yoshiwara

The name of the pleasure quarters in Edo, licensed by the Edo shogunate. It made its start in Nihonbashi, but relocated to Asakusa after the Great Fire of Meireki in 1657. As the largest pleasure quarters in Japan, Yoshiwara encompassed 66,000 m² (1.4 times the size of Tokyo Dome), and accommodated some 3,000 courtesans in its heyday. It was at once the hub of the sex trade and a place for interaction across the social strata. The district became the trendsetting center of urban Edo culture in lifestyle, art, literature, and more. Yoshiwara survived past the Edo period until the Prostitution Prevention Law in 1956 brought it to extinction.

<u>Chapter 1</u>

Ise Mairi

During the Edo period, highways were developed from Edo to various parts of the country. The Edo shogunate prohibited commoners from traveling freely, but pilgrimages to shrines and temples were permitted as acts of praying for the peace of the country. The most iconic place of worship was the Ise Shrine, or Ise Jingu, in Mie prefecture. The Ise

吉原 よしわら

江戸にあった、江戸幕府によって公認された遊郭。はじめは日本橋にあり、1657年の明暦の大火後、浅草へ移転した。日本最大の遊郭で、区画面積は約6万6000㎡（東京ドームの1.4倍）あり、最盛期には約3000人の遊女がいたという。享楽の場であるとともにさまざまな階層の人びとの社交場でもあり、風俗、芸術、文学など、江戸町人文化の中心地となった。江戸時代が終わったのちも存続したが、1956年の売春防止法の成立によって消滅した。

第一章

伊勢まいり いせまいり

江戸時代になると、江戸を起点とした全国各地への街道が整備された。江戸幕府は庶民の自由な旅行を禁じたが、社寺参拝の旅については国家の平和を願う行為とみなされて許可された。社寺参拝の旅の代表が、三重県の伊勢神宮への参拝だった。伊勢神宮は日本の皇室の祖先を祀る神社であり、伊勢神宮への参拝の旅は

Jingu enshrines the ancestors of the Japanese imperial family, and going there to worship was called *Ise Mairi*. For Edoites, the trip to the shrine generally involved a two-week walk on the Tokaido road, a route connecting Edo to Kyoto. Many traveled on to include the rounds of shrines and temples in Kyoto and Nara, stretching their journey to several months.

Karyukai

Karyukai (lit. the flower and willow world) are entertainment districts that are the realm of courtesans and geisha (women who entertain at banquets, singing, dancing, and playing musical instruments). Now that courtesans have disappeared, the term mainly refers to the geisha community.

Hanten

A short, traditional jacket, worn without folding down the collar, mainly used for manual work or for protection against the cold. *Matsuri-banten*, on the other hand, are festival *hanten*, and as the name implies, are more festive in look, the features of which are sometimes shared by a team.

「伊勢まいり」と呼ばれる。江戸の住人が伊勢まいりに出かける場合、一般的には、江戸と京都を結ぶ東海道を歩いてゆき、片道で約2週間かかった。伊勢神宮を参拝したあとに、京都や奈良の社寺巡りをするなど、数か月にわたって旅行する者も多かった。

花柳界 かりゅうかい

遊女や芸者（宴会の場を歌、演奏、踊りなどで盛り上げる女性）のいる社会もしくは場所。現在は遊郭が消滅したため、おもに芸者の社会を指す。

半纏 はんてん

丈の短い上着で、襟を折り返さずに着る。おもに労務のための外着や防寒用として着用する。祭に参加する際に着る「祭半纏」は、参加チームごとに半纏の柄を揃えるなど、華やかなデザインのものもある。

Kirikane

A technique of applying thin strips of gold or silver leaf to sculptures and paintings to express lines and patterns.

Chapter 2

Inro

A men's fashion accessory consisting of small oval containers, stacked in a set of three or five, and held together by a cord that passes through the left and right sides. Hung from the *obi* at the waist. The name, *inro* (lit. seal basket), stems from its intended use as a portable carrier for a personal seal and ink pad, and at times, for pills too. Crafted in *maki-e* lacquer work and other elaborate techniques. A must for a samurai in full dress.

Maki-e

A lacquerware decorating technique that involves painting a motif in lacquer on lacquerware, then sprinkling metal powder such as gold, silver, copper, tin, or colored powder to dry in relief.

切金 きりかね

金箔や銀箔を細長く裁断して、彫刻や絵画に貼り付け、線や文様を表現する技法。

第二章

印籠 いんろう

男性の装身具のひとつ。楕円形の三重もしくは五重の小型容器の左右にひもを通し、腰から提げて携帯した。印章や印肉を入れたことが名の由来で、丸薬を入れることもあった。漆地に蒔絵を施すなど、精巧な細工のものがつくられた。武士が正装した際には必ず腰に提げることをならいとした。

蒔絵 まきえ

漆の技法の一つ。漆で文様を描き、漆が乾かないうちに金、銀、銅、錫などの金属粉や色の粉などを蒔いて付着させる。

Shakudo

Shakudo (lit. red copper) is an alloy of gold, silver, and copper, formed by adding 2-8% gold and 1% silver into copper. When treated with a solution of copper sulfate or copper acetate, the alloy acquires a beautiful purplish black color, which also gives it the names *shikin* (purple gold) and *ukin* (crow gold).

Cloisonné

An enameling technique of applying glaze to a metal surface and firing it at a high temperature to produce a glassy coating. *Shippo*, the Japanese term for cloisonné, meaning seven treasures, or seven jewels, speaks to the gem-like colors of the glaze, a reference to the seven treasures expounded upon in Buddhist scriptures.

Ojime

An *ojime* (lit. cord fastener) is a toggle used to fasten the drawstring of a bag, *kinchaku* pouch, or *inro*. Most *ojime* are spherical and made of materials that include jade, stones, ivory, coral, and metal.

赤銅 しゃくどう

金、銀、銅の合金。銅100に対して、金2〜8、銀1を加えたもの。この合金を硫酸銅、酢酸銅の溶液などで処理をすると紫がかった美しい黒色を示すので、「紫金」「烏金」とも呼ばれる。

七宝 しっぽう

金属の表面に釉薬を塗り、高温で焼いてガラス質の被膜をつくった工芸品。名の由来は、釉薬によってさまざまな発色を示す様子が、仏教の経典で説く「七つの宝石」に譬えられたこととされる。

緒締 おじめ

袋、巾着、印籠などの口（開口部）を締める紐を緒という。緒締は、緒を穴に通して口が開かないようにするための道具。緒締の多くは球形で、玉、石、象牙、珊瑚、金属などさまざまな素材でつくられる。

Chapter 3

Dejima Island

An artificial island built by the Edo shogunate in 1634 in the city of Nagasaki in Nagasaki prefecture to accommodate Portuguese traders. The fan-shaped island covered an area of roughly 13,000 m². Its access to land was via a single bridge. In 1641, sometime after the Portuguese were prohibited from entering Japan, the Dutch trading post, located until then in the city of Hirado in Nagasaki prefecture, was moved to Dejima Island, where the Dutch were also assigned to live. Dejima Island served as Japan's only trading center with the West during the period of national seclusion (1639-1853) when the Edo shogunate closed its doors to the world. The land was reclaimed during the Meiji period to merge into Nagasaki.

Kinkarakawa

Kinkarakawa, or gilded leather, is leather that is embossed or molded to produce raised designs, upon which metal foil is applied. The technique, prevalent in Spain from the 14th to 17th centuries, subsequently spread throughout Europe. Dutch gilded leather, imported during the Edo

第三章

出島 でじま

1634年に江戸幕府がポルトガル人を居住させるために長崎（長崎県長崎市）に築造した人工島。扇形をしており、面積は約1万3000㎡、陸とは1本の橋のみで連絡されていた。ポルトガル人の渡航が禁止された後、1641年に平戸（長崎県平戸市）にあったオランダ人の商館を出島に移して、オランダ人の居住地とした。江戸幕府が鎖国していた時期（1639〜1853）の西洋との唯一の貿易地となり、明治時代になると埋め立てられた。

金唐革 きんからかわ

革に型または打出しによって文様を浮き出させ、そこに金鍍金を施したもの。14〜17世紀にスペインで栄え、その後、ヨーロッパ各国でつくられた。江戸時代の日本にはオランダの金唐革が輸入され、非常に高価な素材として珍重された。

period, was highly expensive and highly prized.

Kaishi

Paper that can be folded and carried around for personal needs. Their uses are wide. They are handy for cleaning off surfaces, as well as for jotting down lyrics when composing a poem (or song). *Kaishi-ire* are *fukuromono* specifically designated to store *kaishi*.

Kiribame

A metalwork technique in which a design is cut out of a thin metal sheet. A different colored piece of metal (*irogane*) is soldered to the cutwork to fill the opening. When the same technique is applied to fabric, cutouts are filled with different fabrics.

Oshi-e

Oshi-e is a textile craft, sometimes called padded collage. Cotton wadding is placed on thick paper that has been cut into the shape of a person, flower, or bird. Each wadded figure is wrapped in fabric or *washi*. They are mounted together on a backing to create a three-dimensional collage effect.

懐紙 かいし

外出の時などに、身だしなみとして、たたんで懐中に入れて持ち歩く紙。懐紙は、汚れを拭き取ったり、即興で歌を詠むときに文字を書いたりするなど、用途はさまざま。「懐紙入れ」は懐紙を入れるための専用の袋物。

切嵌 きりばめ

金工技術の一つ。薄くのばした金属の板に透し彫りをほどこし、透いた部分に別の色の金属板（色金）を嵌め込む。布にほどこす場合は、布地の一部を切り抜いて、その部分に同じ形の異なる種類の布を嵌め込む。

押絵 おしえ

布細工の一種。人物や花鳥の形に切り抜いた厚紙に綿をのせ、和紙や布でくるむ。それらを貼り重ねて立体的な絵柄をつくる。

Tsuzure-ori

Tsuzure-ori, or nail weaving, is a tapestry weaving technique that hides the warp (vertical) threads and produces a pattern with the colored weft (horizontal) threads only.

Chapter 4

Bekko

Bekko, or tortoiseshell, is the processed shell of the hawksbill, a species of sea turtle that lives in the tropical waters of the Atlantic, Pacific, and Indian oceans. Tortoiseshell is translucent and shiny, mottled in yellowish brown and black. Highly prized for the production of decorative artwork and luxury items, hawksbill tortoises fell prey to overhunting and are now protected as a critically endangered species.

Oiran

A high-ranking courtesan in the Yoshiwara pleasure quarters. Called *tayu* in the early Edo period, the designation later changed to *oiran* from the mid-Edo period. The *oiran* reserved the right to choose her customer, while the customer paid a princely sum to win her over.

綴れ織 つづれおり

織物の技法の一つ。縦糸を隠して、色のついた横糸だけで模様をつくる。

第四章

鼈甲 べっこう

大西洋、太平洋、インド洋の熱帯海域に生息するタイマイ（ウミガメの一種）の甲羅を加工したもの。鼈甲は半透明で光沢を帯び、黄褐色の部分と黒色の部分がまだらになっている。工芸品や実用品の高価な素材として珍重されたためにタイマイは乱獲の対象となり、現在は絶滅危惧種に指定され、保護活動が行われている。

花魁 おいらん

吉原遊郭における上級の遊女。江戸時代の初期は、上級の遊女は「太夫」と呼ばれたが、江戸中期頃より花魁と呼ばれるようになった。花魁は客を選ぶ権利があり、花魁のなじみ客になるためにはたいへんな費用がかかった。

Ohaguro

Ohaguro, or teeth blackening, was a part of the beauty routine. Teeth blackening has existed in cultures around the world, and is said to have been part of the Japanese lifestyle from over 1,500 years ago. Although of unconfirmed origin, theory exists that the *ohaguro* custom crossed over from the Korean Peninsula. Initially, upper class men and women dyed their teeth, but in the Edo period, only women blackened their teeth to signify their married status. Since black cannot be dyed into other colors, *ohaguro* became a symbol of female chastity. Still, courtesans in Yoshiwara, though single, blackened their teeth. The government banned the practice in the Meiji period (1868-1912), although a portion of women in mainstream Japanese society blackened their teeth until the mid-20th century.

Biidoro

The old name for glass or glassware, derived from the Portuguese *vidro*. Glass production was introduced by the Portuguese and Dutch who arrived in Nagasaki at the end of the Muromachi period (1336-1573).

第五章

お歯黒 おはぐろ

歯を黒く染める化粧法。歯を黒く染める風習は世界各地で行われたが、日本では1500年以上前から行われていたといわれる。その起源は朝鮮半島からの渡来説などがあるが定かではない。お歯黒は、当初は上流階級の男女の化粧法として行われていたが、江戸時代になると女性のみが、既婚者のしるしとして行うようになる。黒はほかの色に染まらないことから、女性の貞節を象徴するものとなった。ただし、独身であっても吉原の遊女はお歯黒をした。明治時代（1868～1912）になり、政府によってお歯黒は禁止されたが、庶民の一部では20世紀の半ばごろまでお歯黒をする女性がいた。

ビードロ びーどろ

ガラスまたはガラス製品の古い呼び名で、ポルトガル語が語源。室町時代（1336～1573）の末期に長崎に来たポルトガル人やオランダ人がガラスの製法を伝えた。

Chapter 6

Nanban Trade

Trade that was carried on mainly with Portugal and Spain for about 100 years. More specifically, the period of *nanban* trade lasted from mid-16th century till the Edo period in 1639 when Japan declared its national seclusion policy. *Nanban* (lit. southern barbarian) was a term that referred to Portugal and Spain, which possessed colonies in Southeast Asia. Likewise, their trading ships were called *nanban* ships, their ports of call centering mainly on Nagasaki and other points in Kyushu. The traders brought with them guns, gunpowder, raw silk, and leather. Japan, in exchange, included silver, swords, lacquerware, and marine products among its exports. The arrival of the *nanban* ships was perceived as an intent to evangelize Christianity. Christianity was subsequently banned and became one of Japan's reasons for seclusion.

南蛮貿易
なんばんぼうえき

16世紀の中頃から江戸時代の鎖国（1639年）まで約100年間続いた、おもにポルトガルとスペインとの貿易。当時の日本は東南アジアに植民地をもつポルトガルやスペインを南蛮と呼び、その交易船を南蛮船と呼んだ。南蛮船は長崎をはじめとした九州の港におもに来航し、鉄砲・火薬・生糸・皮革などをもたらした。日本からは銀・刀剣・漆器・海産物などを輸出した。南蛮船の来航は、キリスト教の布教も目的としていたため、その後、キリスト教は禁教とされ、鎖国の原因になった。

Appendix

Museums
to Visit

付録

訪ねてみたい美術館

Fukuromono Museum

Since the Edo period, the Tokyo ward of Sumida-ku has been a prosperous area for the manufacturing of household items and decorative accessories. Founded in 1914 and located in Ryogoku (Sumida-ku, Tokyo), Azumaya is a shop specializing in the production of *fukuromono* and other small leather goods. To commemorate its 90th anniversary, the shop opened the Fukuromono Museum in 2004. About 100 items are on display, including *tabako-ire*, *hakoseko*, *kami-ire*, and other *fukuromono* made between the Edo and Taisho period (1912-26), as well as manufacturing tools such as manual sewing machines. In the section of the museum introducing the history of Azumaya, products exported overseas after the war are displayed, and visitors can touch a piece of actual cowhide, the material used for the products.

袋物博物館

　東京都墨田区は江戸時代以来、生活用品や装飾小物などのものづくりが盛んな地域。墨田区両国にある「東屋」は1914年創業の袋物・革小物製造専門店で、2004年に創業90年を記念して袋物博物館を開設した。江戸時代から大正時代にかけてつくられた煙草入れ、筥迫、紙入れなどの袋物を中心に、手動ミシンなどの製作道具などを含む約100点を展示公開している。東屋の歴史を紹介するコーナーでは戦後に海外へ輸出していた商品などを展示し、製品の素材である実際の牛革1枚に触れることもできる。

Exhibition Room
展示室

Address: 1-1-7 Ryogoku, Sumida-ku, Tokyo
Telephone: +81 (0)3-3631-6353
Opening Hours: Weekdays 13:00-16:00
 (Saturdays and Sundays by reservation only)
Admission: Free
Closed: National holidays, Golden Week,
New Year and summer holidays

———

住所：東京都墨田区両国1-1-7
電話：03-3631-6353
営業時間：平日13：00〜16：00（土・日は予約）
入館料：無料
休み：祝日、GW、年末年始、夏季休業期間
URL: azumaya.bz/museum/

Beni Museum

Beni Museum is run by Isehan Honten, a shop that has been making and selling *beni* since the Edo period. The various resources displayed in the museum introduce *beni* making techniques handed down since Isehan Honten's founding in 1825, as well as the history and culture of makeup. Room 1 in the permanent exhibition, "About *Beni*," explains how *beni* is made and the customs surrounding *beni* through models, videos, and other related materials. Room 2, "History of Makeup," looks back at the transformation of makeup in Japan through makeup tools, ukiyo-e prints and other illustrative resources. The company also offers *beni* making workshops and visitors can experience the application of *komachi-beni*, a product manufactured using traditional techniques.

紅ミュージアム

　江戸時代創業の、紅の製造・販売会社「伊勢半本店」が運営する資料館。1825年の創業時から受け継いできた紅づくりの技と、化粧の歴史や文化を数々の資料とともに公開している。常設展示室1は「紅を知る」をテーマに、紅づくりや、紅にまつわる習俗を模型や動画、関連資料で紹介。常設展示室2は「〈化粧〉の歩み」をテーマに、化粧道具や浮世絵などの絵画資料によって日本の化粧の歩みをふりかえる。伝統の技法で製造した同社製品「小町紅」の紅つけ体験や、紅を使ったワークショップなども開催している。

Exhibition Room
展示室

Makeup Tools, Edo Period
化粧道具　江戸時代

Dissolving
Komachi-beni
「小町紅」の紅溶き

Colored *Oshiroi*, Meiji to Showa Period
色付き白粉他　明治〜昭和時代

Introduction to *Beni* Making
紅づくりの展示

Address: 1F, K's Minami Aoyama Building,
6-6-20 Minami Aoyama, Minato-ku, Tokyo
Telephone: +81 (0)3-5467-3735
Opening Hours: 10:00-17:00 (Last entry 16:30)
Admission: Free
Closed: Sundays, Mondays, shop's founding
anniversary (July 7), year-end and New Year
holidays

———

住所：東京都港区南青山6-6-20 K's南青山ビル1F
電話：03-5467-3735
営業時間：10：00～17：00（入館は16：30まで）
入館料：無料
休み：日曜日、月曜日、創業記念日（7月7日）、年末年始
URL: www.isehanhonten.co.jp/museum/

Tobacco & Salt Museum

The Tobacco & Salt Museum is dedicated to the history and cultures surrounding tobacco and salt, goods that were once protected by a government monopoly in Japan. The museum collects resources, conducts research, and introduces a broad range of history and culture pertaining to tobacco and salt. In the permanent exhibition room, "History and Culture of Tobacco," tobacco related resources from around the world and Japan are on display. The "Tobacco Culture in the Edo Period" space features the life-size replicas of Edo period tobacco and *tabako-ire* shops. The museum holds a large collection of Edo period *kiseru*, *tabako-ire*, *tabako-bon*, and ukiyo-e prints related to smoking culture, which are displayed in permanent and special exhibitions.

たばこと塩の博物館

　かつては国の専売品であった、たばこと塩の歴史と文化をテーマとする博物館。たばこと塩に関する資料の収集、調査・研究を行い、その歴史と文化を広く紹介している。常設展示室「たばこの歴史と文化」では、世界と日本のたばこに関する資料を展示。江戸時代のたばこ文化の展示スペースには、江戸時代のたばこ屋とたばこ入れ屋が復元展示されている。江戸時代のきせる、たばこ入れ、たばこ盆、喫煙文化に関する浮世絵などを多数所蔵し、常設展や特別展で公開している。

Tobacco & Salt Museum
たばこと塩の博物館

Tobacco Cultures of the World
世界のたばこ文化

Edo Period *Tabako-ire* Shop (replica)

江戸時代のたばこ入れ屋 (復元)

Modern Tobacco Culture
近現代のたばこ文化

Address: 1-16-3 Yokokawa, Sumida-ku, Tokyo
Telephone: +81 (0)3-3622-8801
Opening Hours: 11:00-17:00 (Last entry 16:30)
Admission fee: 100 yen
Closed: Mondays (when a national or substitute holiday falls on a Monday, the museum is closed on the following day instead), year-end and New Year holidays (possibility of other temporary closures)

———

住所：東京都墨田区横川 1-16-3
電話：03-3622-8801
営業時間：10:00〜17:00 (入館は16:30まで)
入館料：100円
休み：月曜日 (月曜日が祝日、振替休日の場合は直後の平日)、年末年始、臨時休館あり
URL：www.tabashio.jp

平野英夫　ひらの・ひでお
1947年、東京日本橋生まれ。
生家は明治時代から続く袋物商で、
都立工芸高校金属科卒業後ジュエリーデザイナー、
クラフトマンとなる。カルチャースクール講師、
各種講演のほか、『火消し風俗 伊達姿』（芳賀書店）、
『嚢物の世界 江戸小物のデザイン』（求龍堂）など
豪華本の著書多数。掲載作品をはじめ自身の5千点にのぼる
江戸小物や浮世絵コレクションの展覧会をサントリー美術館、
日本橋髙島屋（いずれも東京）などで開催。

編集協力
内田和浩

写真撮影
黒石あみ（小学館）

装丁・本文デザイン
金田一亜弥　髙畠なつみ（金田一デザイン）

英訳
Mae Nagai

和文校正
兼古和昌

協力
日本児童教育振興財団 FAJE

Bilingual Guide to Japan
EDO ACCESSORIES

江戸小物バイリンガルガイド

2021年12月21日　初版　第1刷発行
2024年 5 月27日　　　　第2刷発行

監　修　平野英夫
発行者　斎藤　満
発行所　株式会社小学館
　　　　〒101－8001
　　　　東京都千代田区一ツ橋2－3－1
　　　　編集03－3230－5563　販売03－5281－3555

印刷所　大日本印刷株式会社
製本所　株式会社若林製本工場
DTP　　株式会社昭和ブライト

編　集　矢野文子（小学館）